Proverbs

Volume 2

DISCOVER TOGETHER BIBLE STUDY SERIES

Leader's guides are available at www.discovertogetherseries.com

A Discover Together
BIBLE STUDY

Proverbs

*Discovering Ancient Wisdom
for a Postmodern World
Volume 2*

Sue Edwards

Kregel
Publications

Proverbs: Discovering Ancient Wisdom for a Postmodern World, Volume 2
© 2012 by Sue Edwards

Published by Kregel Publications, a division of Kregel, Inc., P.O. Box 2607, Grand Rapids, MI 49501.

Previously published by Kregel Publications as *Proverbs: Ancient Wisdom for a Postmodern World, Volume 2*, © 2007 by Sue Edwards.

All Scripture quotations, unless otherwise indicated, are taken from the Holy Bible, New International Version®, NIV®. Copyright © 1973, 1978, 1984, 2011 by Biblica, Inc.™ Used by permission of Zondervan. All rights reserved worldwide. www.zondervan.com

Scripture quotations marked KJV are from the King James Version.

ISBN 978-0-8254-4308-4

Printed in the United States of America

12 13 14 15 16 / 5 4 3 2 1

Contents

How to Get the Most Out of a Discover Together Bible Study

Women today need Bible study to keep balanced, focused, and Christ-centered in their busy worlds. The tiered questions in *Proverbs: Discovering Ancient Wisdom for a Postmodern World, Volume 2* allow you to choose a depth of study that fits your lifestyle, which may even vary from week to week, depending on your schedule.

Just completing the basic questions will require about one and a half hours per lesson, and will provide a basic overview of the text. For busy women, this level offers in-depth Bible study with a minimum time commitment.

"Digging Deeper" questions are for those who want to, and make time to, probe the text even more deeply. Answering these questions may require outside resources such as an atlas, Bible dictionary, or concordance; you may be asked to look up parallel passages for additional insight; or you may be encouraged to investigate the passage using an interlinear Greek-English text or *Vine's Expository Dictionary*. This deeper study will challenge you to learn more about the history, culture, and geography related to the Bible, and to grapple with complex theological issues and differing views. Some with teaching gifts and an interest in advanced academics will enjoy exploring the depths of a passage, and might even find themselves creating outlines and charts and writing essays worthy of seminarians!

This inductive Bible study is designed for both individual and group discovery. You will benefit most if you tackle each week's lesson on your own, and then meet with other women to share insights, struggles, and aha moments. Bible study leaders will find free, downloadable leader's guides for each study, along with general tips for leading small groups, at www.discovertogetherseries.com.

Through short video clips, Sue Edwards shares personal insights to enrich your Bible study experience. You can watch these as you work through each lesson on your own, or your Bible study leader may want your whole study group to view them when you meet together. For ease of individual

viewing, a QR code, which you can simply scan with your smartphone, is provided in each lesson. Or you can go to www.discovertogetherseries.com and easily navigate until you find the corresponding video title. Woman-to-woman, these clips are meant to bless, encourage, and challenge you in your daily walk.

Choose a realistic level of Bible study that fits your schedule. You may want to finish the basic questions first, and then "dig deeper" as time permits. Take time to savor the questions, and don't rush through the application. Watch the videos. Read the sidebars for additional insight to enrich the experience. Note the optional passage to memorize and determine if this discipline would be helpful for you. Do not allow yourself to be intimidated by women who have more time or who are gifted differently.

Make your Bible study—whatever level you choose—top priority. Consider spacing your study throughout the week so that you can take time to ponder and meditate on what the Holy Spirit is teaching you. Do not make other appointments during the group Bible study. Ask God to enable you to attend faithfully. Come with an excitement to learn from others and a desire to share yourself and your journey. Give it your best, and God promises to join you on this adventure that can change your life.

Why Study Proverbs?

A proverb is a short, pithy couplet that teaches truth in a memorable way. Here are two examples:

Anxiety weighs down the heart,
  but a kind word cheers it up. (Proverbs 12:25)

If anyone loudly blesses their neighbor early in the morning,
  it will be taken as a curse. (Proverbs 27:14)

These short, pithy sayings begin in chapter 10 and end in chapter 29. The book of Proverbs is structured like a sandwich: these brief, memorable sayings are sandwiched between discourses at the beginning and at the end.

Here's another way to look at the organization:

Chapters 1–9   Incentives to seek wisdom from King Solomon
Chapters 10–29   Proverbs
Chapters 30–31   Insight on wisdom from Agur and King Lemuel's mother

 Introduction to Studying Proverbs (*7:42 minutes*).

WHAT YOU NEED TO KNOW ABOUT PROVERBS

Proverbs are *principles* that are true in general terms. They show us the way the world works and how to live wisely in it. If we live by wisdom

principles, we will not bring calamity on our heads by our own foolish actions and attitudes. Foolishness is the source of many people's problems. When we are our own worst enemies, we bring problems upon ourselves either by being unaware of how the world works or by ignoring what we know.

Proverbs are not *promises*. If we interpret proverbs as promises made to individuals, we're guilty of saying that God promises us something that he has not promised at all, and we confuse people regarding the Bible. It is crucial that we interpret the Bible in the way that the author intended.

A proverb is a wise saying—a few words pregnant with meaning. We must examine each word carefully and then dig for the overall meaning. When Benjamin Franklin coined the secular proverb, "A stitch in time saves nine," he was not promising that if you stitch up a hem before it unravels, it will never unravel again. He was explaining that if we attend to a situation early, we'll most likely encounter fewer problems later. Franklin was using figurative language to paint a picture of the way the world works. Solomon was his predecessor.

When mothers read the proverb, "Train up a child in the way he should go: and when he is old, he will not depart from it" (Proverbs 22:6 KJV), it's tempting to insist that God promises all prodigals will return. And God may give a mother that assurance. But God never makes that promise on the basis of this particular proverb. To insist that he has is to use bad interpretive principles. Instead, this proverb tells us that parents who do their best to understand their children and raise them in a godly home are *more likely* to see prodigals return to the faith than are those parents who never instructed their children in the first place. But turning to God is ultimately the child's choice. God does not override free choice for anyone. That's a principle he set in place from the foundation of the world.

Our task is to decipher the proverbs in order to learn timeless lessons about life, and then to live in light of their truth.

Proverbs' purpose is to propel us into a relationship with God so we might live out the truths he shows us in this guidebook. They're valuable principles, but they are not promises. When we interpret proverbs as promises, we mishandle God's Word and mislead ourselves and others— and that gets us into trouble!

A NOTE ON BIBLE TRANSLATIONS

The 2011 New International Version (NIV) is the version used throughout this study. Because it uses gender neutral language where that fits with the intent of the original text, the author recommends this version for clarity. If you use another version, you'll need to keep in mind that the 1984 NIV and many other standard Bible translations use "man" and "sons" to represent the human race in general.

Raising Up the Next Generation

God's work on the earth is only one generation away from extinction. Is this statement true? Yes and no. We have a promise from God that his church will endure until he returns (Matthew 16:18). Nevertheless, it is our privilege and responsibility to woo, win, and equip the generation behind us. If we fail, those following us will be hindered and weakened in impacting the generations to come. The spiritual health and eternal destinies of countless souls depend on our diligence.

Raising up the next generation takes multiple forms: parenting and grandparenting, building into the lives of children and youth, and mentoring other women. We are all called to raise up the next generation in some way.

The book of Proverbs is packed with principles to help us. Many proverbs speak specifically to parenting, but we can glean principles to help us mentor youth, college students, or women. Take the lessons and apply them to your own calling. If you are a mother or grandmother, there is a gold mine of wisdom to help you raise your children. If you are without biological children, you are also needed to come alongside young people or younger women in your extended family, church, or workplace. It is everybody's work! And what joy to see the generation behind us take up the baton for our God.

OPTIONAL

Memorize Psalm 78:2–4

I will open my mouth with a parable; I will utter hidden things; things from of old—things we have heard and known, things our ancestors have told us. We will not hide them from their descendants; we will tell the next generation the praiseworthy deeds of the Lord, his power, and the wonders he has done.

I came to faith in my mid-twenties and I was a mess. But women in the Bible study I attended remothered me for almost fifteen years, showing me how much God loved me and guiding me with tenderness and wisdom. They were "Jesus with skin" to me and I am eternally grateful. Now I want to do the same for women that God brings across my path who are looking for guidance. But I'm just one woman. We need an army of mentors! Please consider how God might use you to change others' lives, the way my life was impacted.   —Sue

1. What did God tell Moses as he prepared him for ministry (Exodus 3:15)? Are you ministering to anyone in the next generation? A child? A young person? A younger woman in your group, office, or neighborhood? If so, who? If not, ask God to reveal someone you might influence, showing him or her the wonder of your God.

2. What happened to the Israelites in Judges 2:10–15? What might happen in the lives of the next generation if we fail them? What impact would there be on us and our nation?

3. What did God instruct the Jews to do in Psalm 48:12–14? What principle can we apply today as we mentor the next generation?

4. What is the special admonition to older women (Psalm 71:18)? Why are they such valuable counselors and trainers of the next generation?

5. The author instructs us to follow his example in Psalm 78:1–7. Can you think of creative ways to "not hide" our love for God and to "tell the next generation"? What could you do this week?

DIGGING DEEPER

Throughout the epistles, we observe Paul mentoring many men and women. Give some examples. Study his methodology. What can you learn to help you be an effective mentor today?

DIGGING DEEPER

Paul wrote his last letter (2 Timothy) to Timothy, his "dear son" in the Lord. This letter reveals Paul's last thoughts before he was executed, as well as fascinating insight into Paul and Timothy's relationship. What can you glean from this little letter about the art of mentoring?

 Mentoring (*4:41 minutes*). Mentoring is as valuable today as ever, but times have changed. Younger women have different expectations of the mentoring relationship than older women.

Although a man may be able to clearly *define* femininity, who could better *model* godly gender characteristics of a woman than a woman? Women need to know what godliness looks like in a feminine body. . . . Feminine perspective balances the masculine perspective that is most often heard in our public church services or from our fathers.
—Beverly Hislop
(*Shepherding*, 26)

DIGGING DEEPER

Examine the relationship of Mary and Elizabeth in Luke 1:39–56. What difference did Elizabeth make in Mary's life? What can you learn from her?

DIGGING DEEPER

Within the pages of the book of Ruth are priceless principles on mentoring. Study Ruth's relationship with her mother-in-law, Naomi. How was Naomi a good model of a mentor? How was she a poor model? Write a guidebook on mentoring from the book of Ruth.

Walk about Zion, go around her, count her towers, consider well her ramparts, view her citadels, that you may tell of them to the next generation.
—Psalm 48:12–13

What kind of women do we need to be to best influence the next generation?

6. What is top priority (Proverbs 9:10)?

7. What else is important (Proverbs 20:7)? Does this mean we must be perfect? What do you think is the general principle? How might you use your imperfections to minister to the next generation?

8. What does a godly mentor seek to attain? What will be the result in the lives of those following behind her (24:3–4)? Who are the "rare and beautiful treasures"?

TWO MENTORING SKILLS

As we build into the lives of the next generation, the Scriptures instruct us to balance encouragement and correction (Ephesians 4:15; 2 Timothy 4:2; Titus 2:15). One without the other creates serious problems—especially in the lives of children. Let's explore these two skills as we invest in the lives of others.

Encouragement

9. What principles can you glean from Deuteronomy 6:6–7 as you mentor the next generation?

> I believe with all my heart that there is the potential for a revival of faith and virtue among women. If Christian women begin to fathom the power of our God-given capacity, develop these God-honoring characteristics, and nurture younger women, perhaps we will see the fruit of righteousness flourish in women in our decade.
> —Susan Hunt
> (*Spiritual Mothering*, 19)

10. *Read Hebrews 10:24–25.* How can you use these principles to build into the lives of those God calls you to mentor? Be specific.

11. How are we to minister to the next generation when they struggle (Proverbs 12:25; Romans 15:1–2)?

12. How might we apply Ephesians 6:4, first to children and then to others we are mentoring? What are some specific ways to "exasperate" others?

13. Proverbs 22:6 is not a promise but a principle that reveals great wisdom for training the next generation. What do you think it means to train others "on the way they should go"? Why is it important to consider the unique differences in those we mentor?

Correction

14. Why is it important to correct those coming behind us (Proverbs 22:15; 29:15)? What is our nature (Psalm 51:5; Ephesians 2:3)?

15. What happens in the end to those who despise correction (Proverbs 5:11–14)?

16. We correct the next generation for their good. Specifically, how will they benefit?

    Proverbs 3:23

    Proverbs 4:8–9

Relating is at the heart of knowing God. Relating is also at the heart of becoming the people of God. Our faith journey is one we make together. Community is the context for our growth, and it is a distinctively Christian concept.
—Julie Gorman
(*Community*, 24)

Proverbs 4:12

17. What is the principle in 29:21? Apply this to your mentoring relationships.

18. Why is it important to know well those you mentor before you offer correction (9:7–9)?

19. When will correction work (25:12)? What is the meaning of Solomon's analogy?

20. What should the attitude of our hearts be when we correct others (1 Peter 3:15)?

21. Should we ever give up on those we mentor? What did Jesus say in Luke 17:3–4? Does this mean we should continue to work with someone indefinitely if they are not responsive?

REALISTIC EXPECTATIONS

The best training alone cannot make someone wise. Whether we mentor children or adults, we need to understand that we cannot force anyone to love God or live well. There are many reasons why our mentoring may not be productive. Let's look at several.

22. Consider the people in the following proverbs. How can they negate our training?

Proverbs 10:5b

Proverbs 15:20b

Proverbs 17:21

Proverbs 28:24

Proverbs 29:1

Proverbs 29:3b

23. Ultimately, who is responsible for each person's relationship with God and for the path her life takes? Why is it important to understand this fact as we raise up the next generation?

24. Nevertheless, we are called to build into the next generation to the best of our ability. When we do, often we see the fruit of our labor. What is our hope and often our reward?

One generation commends your works to another; they tell of your mighty acts.
—Psalm 145:4

25. What is the reciprocal relationship expressed in 17:6?

26. Why is mentoring usually such a blessing (23:24–25)?

27. How do we glorify God through our mentoring? Is this reward worth the risk and investment (Psalm 22:30–31; 145:4–7)?

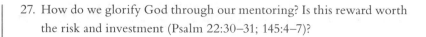

DISCIPLINE AND CORRECTION

Within the family, mentoring takes on the additional functions of providing discipline and correction—a subject on which families have widely differing opinions. The use of spanking, for instance, can provoke controversy, and many health-care and child-care workers are now instructed to view and report it as child abuse. Please discuss these subjects with kindness and listen to the varied opinions. Then allow God to guide your personal views as you minister to children in your care.

28. Read the following verses on "the rod." What did application of "the rod" look like in Solomon's day? What might it look like in our day? According to Solomon, what might this kind of discipline accomplish?

Proverbs 13:24

Proverbs 23:13–14

Proverbs 29:15

29. How and when should physical discipline be administered to children? Are there any dangers? What are important parameters?

30. *Read Proverbs 19:18*. Discuss effective means of discipline and correction beyond physical discipline such as spanking.

Mothers, it's worth it. It's worth it. It's worth every hour of it. It's worth every sleepless night of it. It's worth every moment of counsel.
—Charles Swindoll (*Tale*, 399)

WHAT ABOUT YOU?

As you have worked through this lesson, has God placed someone on your heart that he wants you to mentor? If so, devise a plan to begin investing in her life and put it into action this week.

"Fear" the Lord

Proverbs are practical, pithy sayings that show us how the world works and how to live well in it. But the power to live well comes from the Holy Spirit, knowledge of the truth, and a teachable heart. Proverbs' theme verse captures wisdom's prerequisite: "The fear of the LORD is the beginning of wisdom" (9:10a). What does it mean to "fear" the Lord? It is not running from God in terror, so frightened that we want to hide. Because of Christ's sacrifice on our behalf, we can enter his presence confidently, knowing he loves us.

However, he alone is God—holy, sovereign, and worthy of unending worship, honor, and praise. He is not our buddy, the great Santa Claus in the sky, nor is our relationship casual or careless. Let's explore our relationship with the Creator God to learn what it means to "fear" him in a biblical sense. With a solid understanding of biblical fear, we are humbled and enabled to see life from God's perspective and to live life well.

OPTIONAL

Memorize Proverbs 31:30
Charm is deceptive, and beauty is fleeting; but a woman who fears the LORD is to be praised.

Do you not know? Have you not heard? . . . He sits enthroned above the circle of the earth, and its people are like grasshoppers. He stretches out the heavens like a canopy, and spreads them out like a tent to live in. He brings princes to naught and reduces the rulers of this world to nothing. . . . The LORD is the everlasting God, the Creator of the ends of the earth. He will not grow tired or weary, and his understanding no one can fathom.
—Isaiah 40:21–23, 28

PROBE THE PASSAGE

It is one of the paradoxes of God that we cannot be made new until we admit that we are incapable of remaking ourselves. We may be closest to holiness when we're overwhelmed by the irreparable twistedness of our hearts. That is when miracles start.
—Stephanie Gehring
("Wisdom")

Job was a good man, perhaps a contemporary of Abraham, who had reason to ask God, "Why?" After losing his money, his children, and his health, his wife suggested that he "curse God and die." But Job loved the Lord and wanted to trust him, even in the midst of his suffering. Nevertheless, as his ordeal continued, he began to question God. He accused God of injustice, of not caring. Friends who visited him did not help. They were "prosperity theologians," believing that misfortune was always the result of sin. They accused Job of secret sins and insisted that God would not otherwise have allowed these trials. Under the stress, Job began hammering God with questions, accusing him of being unfair and unloving. In the final chapters of the book of Job, God teaches Job what it means to "fear the Lord."

Read Job 38 and 39 at least five days this week. Ask the Holy Spirit to illuminate the passage for you. Conclude your reading each day by meditating on Job's awakening in 42:1–6 and ask yourself questions:

- What is the main idea of the passages?
- Was there an idea that was particularly striking, causing me to stop and think?
- Why did God record this in the Bible for me?
- How does this impact my life right now and in the future?
- What questions do I have about the passages?
- What does it mean to "fear the Lord"?

Don't be surprised if you don't understand all you read right away. Don't be discouraged if this poetic language is difficult. Simply attempt to discern the gist of what the author says. Keep probing the passage with questions. Record your thoughts each day.

Day 1

DIGGING DEEPER

Read Job 40–42.

DIGGING DEEPER

Read the book of Job. Chart the book, dividing it into subsections and labeling each subsection. How does this overview help you understand the theme of the book? State the theme in a clear sentence. What is one application the Holy Spirit wants to teach you right now?

Whence comes wisdom?. . . First, one must learn to reverence God. "The fear of the Lord is the beginning of wisdom." Not till we have become humble and teachable, standing in awe of God's holiness and sovereignty, acknowledging our own littleness, distrusting our own thoughts, and willing to have our minds turned upside down, can divine wisdom become ours.
—J. I. Packer (*Knowing God*, 91)

Day 2

Day 3

Day 4

Day 5

The word translated as "fear" also connotes awe and respect. It is the recognition that God is much greater than humans, and the acknowledgement that the blessings God gives are gifts, not anything owed anyone. Within the context of the praise of wisdom, "fear of the LORD" also means that a truly wise person recognizes that (1) God alone truly comprehends wisdom; (2) wisdom is a reflection of God as creator; and (3) humans cannot attain wisdom apart from God. The pursuit of wisdom is the quest to know God, and true knowledge of God results in fear, awe, and respect.
—Corinne Carvalho
(*Encountering Ancient Voices*, 386)

LEARNING TO FEAR GOD, FROM PROVERBS

1. The authors of Proverbs repeat the "fear the Lord" theme three times: Proverbs 1:7; 9:10; and 31:30. Ponder the location of these three verses. Why do you think the author placed them where he did?

Resolved, never to do anything which I should be afraid to do if it were the last hour of my life.
—Jonathan Edwards
(1703–1758)

DIGGING DEEPER

Do a word study on the Hebrew word יָרֵא, which we translate "fear." Using a Hebrew-English Bible, a Hebrew lexicon, and *Vine's Expository Dictionary*, discover the different ways this word can be understood. List some passages that include this word and describe the context in which it is used each time.

2. What are some characteristics of people who fear the Lord?

   Proverbs 8:13

When my daughter was in high school, her friend showed me a poem she had written, comparing God to her comb. In the poem, she thanked God that he was always available to her, that she could carry him around in her pocket, and she could get him out if she ever needed help. I realized this sweet girl had no idea who God is. He's not someone you can carry around in your pocket to get you out of a jam. I see too many people who don't understand "the fear of the Lord" today and it affects their lives in immeasurable ways. —Sue

Proverbs 15:33

Proverbs 16:6

Proverbs 19:23

Wise Up (*3:31 minutes*). Have you heard, "Don't make the same mistakes I did"? Have you heeded that sage advice?

 Read Proverbs 30:1–4.

3. What does Agur say about himself?

To fear the Lord is not the same as saying, "I'm scared of the Lord"; the right kind of fear makes us happy, not frightened, and it makes us secure by acknowledging our vulnerability. Fear of the Lord brings this joy because it acknowledges what is most true about human beings: that we are limited, imperfect, and need help.
—Kim Paffenroth
(*In Praise of Wisdom*, 6)

4. What is the answer to the questions he asks?

5. Do you think Agur fears the Lord? What gives you that impression?

DIGGING DEEPER

What is your response to the creation passages in Proverbs (3:19–20; 8:22–31)? How do you feel as you read them?

DIGGING DEEPER

God alone is worthy of our worship. What do these proverbs reveal about him (Proverbs 5:21; 15:3, 11; 16:2, 4; 17:3; 20:27)?

6. What is the warning in 29:25? Do you tend to make this mistake? If so, how has your life been affected? How can you be an overcomer?

This is what the Lord says: "Let not the wise boast of their wisdom or the strong boast of their strength or the rich boast of their riches, but let the one who boasts boast about this: that they have the understanding to know me, that I am the Lord, who exercises kindness, justice and righteousness on earth, for in these I delight," declares the Lord.
—Jeremiah 9:23–24

7. Describe the danger in 24:21–22. What can happen? Do you have a similar personal experience you can share?

8. What are Solomon's instructions in 23:17–18? What do you think he means? What is one specific way you can apply this mandate to your life today?

DO YOU FEAR THE LORD?

9. Now that you have studied Job and Proverbs, what is your perception of "the fear of the Lord"? Do you tend to be careless as you approach Almighty God? Or do you tend to be so afraid of him that you cannot enjoy the relationship? How do you think God wants you to relate to him?

for small group discussion use

Directions for use: During discussion time, the leader will use this guide to lead her group through an analysis of Job 38–39 and 42:1–6.

The book of Job: The book of Job is a poetic book. There is no consensus as to who wrote the book or when. Some scholars believe it was written during the time of Solomon, when wisdom literature flourished. It has been suggested that Job, Elihu, Solomon, or Moses authored this book.

The theme of the book explores the problem of "righteous suffering" and the sovereignty of God. The book presents Job as a real person who is free to ask God, "Why?" But it is also a book that reminds us that God is good and he is free to do as he wills.

To hear what the Holy Spirit is saying to you through these passages, ask some questions to help you observe the facts: Who? What? Where? Why? and How? No detail is too small. God loves for us to dig for treasures in his Word. This process of observing is very important and shouldn't be hurried. It is through this process that you see and discover what the author is saying. Many questions may come to mind as you read and reread. Ask them, write them down, and look up other Scripture references to see what you can find. You may also want to read the passage in another version of the Bible.

What Does the Passage Say?

- *Who* is speaking (chapters 38–39)?

- *Who* is listening (chapters 38–39)?

- *What* details do you observe in these verses (38:1–3)?

- *How* is the scene in chapters 38–39 described?

- *How* does the Lord address Job's suffering?

- *What* can you observe about the Lord in chapters 38–39?

- *What* can you observe about Job's response in 42:1–6?

- *What* key words are in Job's response (42:1–6)?

- *What* else did you observe in this passage?

Now that you have read and thought and questioned and gathered all sorts of facts and clues like an investigative reporter, it's time to move to the next step: interpretation.

―――――――――――― **What Does It Mean?** ――――――――――――

- *Why* do you think the Lord addressed Job as he did in 38:1–3?

- *Why* do you think the Lord answered Job with questions?

- *Why* do you think the Lord didn't address Job's suffering?

- *What* do you think was the Lord's point to all the questions in chapters 38–39?

- *Why* do you think Job responded like he did in 42:1–6?

- *What* do you think Job meant in 42:5?

- *What* do you think Job meant when he said, "I despise myself, and repent in dust and ashes"?

- *What* do you think the main idea is?

These kinds of questions will help you better understand what the author meant in the passage. All of this is key in moving to the next question, "What is the Holy Spirit saying to me personally through this passage?" Here is where you go beyond seeing and understanding to recognizing that God, the Holy Spirit, is speaking to you directly through his Word so you will know how to apply it to your life.

- *What* is the Holy Spirit saying to me in this passage?

- *What* is one way to apply what he's saying to my life (i.e., family, friendships, marriage, work, ministry, social life)?

My prayer is that as you get into God's Word, you will become accustomed to hearing the voice of God through the Holy Spirit.

Cool Down Those Hot Flashes

A Study on Anger and Patience

An auto mechanic cheats you. You overhear a coworker, family member, or acquaintance distort something you said. Your clinging toddler throws a fit as you prepare dinner for special company. Our first reaction is anger . . . our pulse races, muscles tense, a warm sensation shoots up the back of the neck.

Anger is a natural emotion—part of being made in the image of God. God experiences emotion just as we do. The Bible reveals that all three persons of the Godhead exhibit anger:

> *God the Father*: "The wrath of God is being revealed from heaven against all the godlessness and wickedness of people, who suppress the truth by their wickedness" (Romans 1:18).

> *God the Son*: "He looked around at them in anger and [was] deeply distressed at their stubborn hearts" (Mark 3:5).

> *God the Spirit*: "So, as the Holy Spirit says: . . . 'That is why I was angry with that generation'" (Hebrews 3:7, 10).

But God does not sin in his anger, and we are to follow his example. "'In your anger do not sin': Do not let the sun go down while you are still angry" (Ephesians 4:26 quoting Psalm 4:4). God's anger is always a righteous anger. It focuses on injustice and unrighteousness and it is *never* out of control. Nor does God have a short fuse. "You are a forgiving God, gracious and compassionate, *slow* to anger and abounding in love" (Nehemiah 9:17, emphasis added).

A passionate response to life sometimes involves righteous anger. But God demands that we overcome unrighteous, selfish anger and replace it with patience and mercy. Only then can we be wise women, sowing health, peace, and joy in our relationships and showing the world how God's people live.

Overcoming unrighteous anger, irritation, and annoyance is a tall

order, a lifelong endeavor. We are tempted every day. Nevertheless, God expects us to become patient, gentle women in control of our emotions. He has given us all we need for the task—his Spirit and his Word. Let's dig into Proverbs and overcome this obstacle together.

 Chill! (*4:09 minutes*). Remember this story the next time you're frustrated about others making you late!

A PORTRAIT OF ANGER

Anger is an acid that can do more harm to the vessel in which it's stored than to anything on which it's poured.
—*Baptist Beacon*
(Cory, *Quotable*, 118)

1. How do people typically act when they are angry (Proverbs 14:16–17; 27:4; 29:22)?

He who angers you conquers you.
—Sister Elizabeth Kenny's mother (Kenny, *And They Shall Walk*, 13)

2. People express their anger in different ways. Some hold it in, others rage out loud. How do you express anger? What are healthy ways to express anger? Unhealthy ways?

3. Describe the ruler's rage in 19:12. Have you ever witnessed a similar scene? Can you recall a time when you acted this way?

The word *patience* comes from two Greek words meaning *stay under*.

4. What else is typical of a quick-tempered fool (12:16)?

One moment of patience may ward off a great disaster; one moment of impatience may ruin a whole life.
                    —Chinese proverb
            (Cory, *Quotable*, 276)

5. What can you expect if you go to court with an angry person (29:9)?

6. How will an angry person affect the community (29:8)?

DIGGING DEEPER

Although Moses was God's man, he reaped some serious consequences because of his inability to control his anger in Numbers 20. What happened? What price did he pay? What clues in the text suggest why Moses might have been angry? Have you ever let this happen to you?

DIGGING DEEPER

Often the Bible says that God is slow to anger and abounding in love (Exodus 34:6; Numbers 14:18; Nehemiah 9:17; Psalms 86:15; 103:8). Nevertheless, he hates sin and his wrath will spill out on the world one day. Study the seven seals, trumpets, and bowls in Revelation 6–18 to learn more about God's terrifying righteous anger.

7. Solomon uses figurative language to show us the damage anger can do. Can you decipher these word pictures and explain what he means?

Proverbs 27:3

Proverbs 30:33

Anger, like fire, finally dies out—after leaving a path of destruction.
—Author unknown
(Cory, *Quotable*, 24)

DEALING WITH ANGRY PEOPLE

8. What is Solomon's counsel concerning friends given to anger (Proverbs 22:24–25)? Why? Can you share a personal example? (No names, please.)

9. What would you do if you met a mother bear whose cub was kidnapped? What should you do if you see an angry fool (17:12)? Why?

10. How does a wise woman interact with angry people (15:1)? Has this ever worked for you? If so, please share.

DIGGING DEEPER

Jacob and Leah had a daughter named Dinah who was raped by a Canaanite prince. How did her brothers respond? What were the consequences? What can we learn about rash decisions (Genesis 34)?

11. What is the warning in Proverbs 19:19? Have you ever "bailed" out a friend, only to see him or her commit the offense again? Why is it important to follow Solomon's counsel with loved ones in trouble?

The key to everything is patience. You get the chicken by hatching the egg, not by smashing it open.
—Arnold Glasow
(1905–1998),
American humorist

12. What is the first step in overcoming this powerful emotion (14:16)? What does this mean?

Avoiding anger is like shutting off all electricity to your house because you're worried about being electrocuted. Oh, you might be safe from electrocution inside your house, but you're going to miss out on a lot of benefits of electricity. Anger—as God intends—is holy. If it's part of who God is and how he expresses himself—and God is definitely angry sometimes—an emotion is holy as long as we're not messing it up. We can sin in anger, but God can't, which means anger doesn't have to be sinful.
—Susan Lawrence
(*Pure Emotion*, 102)

13. In 16:32, Solomon says that it is better to conquer the emotion of anger than to conquer a whole city. Do you agree? Which is more difficult?

DIGGING DEEPER

How does James suggest we learn to overcome anger (James 1:19–20)?

14. We cannot overcome anger by an act of our will. What is required for victory (Galatians 5:13–26)? Summarize these verses in a sentence.

15. What does Paul suggest in Ephesians 4:26? What do you think he means?

16. What is our "glory" in Proverbs 19:11? What is Solomon saying? Have you learned this lesson? If so, suggest ways to help others.

17. What does a fool do in 29:11? How are we to be different? What are some practical ways to do this?

Thomas Edison was a man of patience. No test that exists today screens for that.
—Dr. Morris Stein, professor of psychology

18. How will others describe us if we learn to control our anger (17:27)?

The LORD is a jealous and avenging God; the LORD takes vengeance and is filled with wrath. The LORD takes vengeance on his foes and vents his wrath against his enemies. The Lord is slow to anger but great in power; the LORD will not leave the guilty unpunished. His way is in the whirlwind and the storm, and clouds are the dust of his feet. . . . The mountains quake before him and the hills melt away. The earth trembles at his presence, the world and all who live in it. Who can withstand his indignation? Who can endure his fierce anger?
—Nahum 1:2–3, 5–6

19. What can happen if we are impulsive (19:2)?

THE BENEFITS OF OVERCOMING ANGER

And soon my prayers were answered, first when patience miraculously descended like soft chick-yellow parachute silk. Before, I had been fretting and pacing while waiting to hear from the doctor. But patience is when God—or something—makes the now a little roomier.
—Anne Lamott
(*Traveling Mercies*, 167)

20. What will we gain by developing a patient, gentle attitude (14:29)?

21. What will we be able to do (15:18)? Do others perceive you this way?

HOW DO YOU HANDLE ANGER?

How much do you want victory over anger in your life? Victory requires honesty, analysis, and dependence on God to help us change.

22. Recall the last time you were very angry. What prompted the feeling? How did you respond? How did you feel afterward?

We struggle with patience because patience signifies dependence. We're dependent on God. Yes, we have choices . . . and one of those choices—applied on a daily basis—is whether or not to acknowledge our dependence on God. Whether or not to accept our position as the created, acknowledging God as the Creator. Without settling the dependence issue, we're not going to settle the patience issue.
—Susan Lawrence
(*Pure Emotion*, 103)

23. What could you do to respond differently the next time?

Do not take revenge, my dear friends, but leave room for God's wrath, for it is written: "It is mine to avenge; I will repay," says the Lord. On the contrary: "If your enemy is hungry, feed him; if he is thirsty, give him something to drink. In doing this, you will heap burning coals on his head." Do not be overcome by evil, but overcome evil with good.
—Romans 12:19–21

24. Anger generates energy and, if we lose control, we often strike out at the cause of our anger. Instead, what are some constructive ways to release the pent-up energy we feel?

25. If you have been successful in controlling your anger, share some practical tips with the group.

26. Anger affects how we appear.

    • Describe the person you are when anger controls you. What is your demeanor? Your face? Your voice? Your body language? What are you like?

    • Describe the person you are when you control anger. What is your demeanor? Your face? Your voice? Your body language? What are you like?

27. With God, you can overcome anger. How would your life be different? How would your relationships be affected? What will you do to become an overcomer?

I like the attitude of the preacher who refused to take revenge. He said, "I'm not going to get even. I'm going to tell God on you!"
—Author unknown
(Swindoll, *Tale*, 269)

In the Shadow of Shaddai

A Study on Security

Our fallen world is a dangerous place: AIDS, nuclear threats, war, sex trafficking, 9/11, Columbine, pornography, loneliness, aging, cancer, accidents, and betrayal. Turn on the news, pick up a newspaper, take in a movie—you've got a front-row seat. Is it possible to find a sense of security, even in the midst of these unsettling circumstances? Does God want us to live in fear? Where can we go to find safety and security?

The world has never been a safe place—yet God promises security in him. We live in this tension every day. How can we learn to face life's realities with courage and peace, entrusting ourselves and our loved ones to a God who loves us dearly? Let's find out.

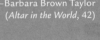

OPTIONAL

Memorize Psalm 91:1–2

Whoever dwells in the shelter of the Most High will rest in the shadow of the Almighty. I will say of the LORD, "He is my refuge and my fortress, my God, in whom I trust."

PROBE THE PASSAGE

Commit to reading Psalm 91 at least five days this week. Ask the Holy Spirit to illuminate the passage for you before you read each day. During the week, as you meditate on the passage, ask yourself questions about the psalm:

- What is the mood of the psalmist as he writes?
- What names of God does he use?
- What is going on in the psalmist's life?
- What is the main point of the psalm?
- Was there an idea that was particularly striking, causing me to stop and think?
- Why did God record this in the Bible for me?
- How does this impact my life right now and in the future?
- What questions do I have about the psalm?

Don't be surprised if nothing jumps out at you right away. Don't be discouraged if you don't understand all you read. Be patient and probe the passage with questions. Record your thoughts each day.

Deep suffering makes theologians of us all.
—Barbara Brown Taylor
(*Altar in the World*, 42)

Day 1

Day 2

Day 3

All of us were born with a
natural tendency to attach
ourselves to a savior and worship him. To see him high and
lifted up. That's why it had
better be Christ. We are safe
with no other. Isaiah 43:11
says it succinctly: "I, even
I, am the LORD, and apart
from me there is no savior."
—Beth Moore
(*Get Out of That Pit*, 107)

Day 4

Day 5

Security (*4:42 minutes*). Are you able to rest in the security of God's arms, whatever comes? When situations frustrate your plans, do you relax or rant?

SOLOMON ON SAFETY

1. Enjoying security and safety does not necessarily mean bad things won't happen. What is the promise in Proverbs 14:32? Discuss the implications.

2. The gift of security and protection in this life comes at a cost. What is our part?

   Proverbs 1:33

   Proverbs 2:8

Grace gave [Paul] courage to be who he was. Grace energized him to accomplish what he did. By realizing that he did not deserve and could never earn the privileges given him, Paul was freed to be exactly who he was and do precisely what he was called to do. Grace became his silent partner, his constant traveling companion, his invisible security.
—Charles Swindoll
(*Grace Awakening*, 201)

Proverbs 10:9

Proverbs 28:18

Proverbs 28:26

Proverbs 30:5–6

3. What are the wonderful benefits when we walk in wisdom (3:21–26)?
   Which do you need most right now?

4. What is an additional blessing for mothers (14:26)? Why do you think this is true?

5. What are we to do when we sense danger (18:10; 22:3)? Discuss some practical ways to do this.

6. What is the warning in 29:25? (See also Luke 12:4–5.) How can "people-pleasing" put us in danger?

Can a mother forget the baby at her breast and have no compassion on the child she has borne? Though she may forget, I will not forget you! See, I have engraved you on the palms of my hands.
—God (Isaiah 49:15–16)

DIGGING DEEPER

Study Matthew 6:25–34 where Jesus teaches principles to help us rest in him. Note his use of questions. Write out the main idea and subpoints. How can these words help you right now?

DIGGING DEEPER

Luke 8:22–56 contains a series of teachings on overcoming fear. Dissect the section, labeling each story and its relationship to the concept of fear. How does Jesus use these accounts to teach us different lessons on trusting him?

Joy isn't grounded in our circumstances; it is grounded in the unchanging character of God.
—Carolyn Custis James
(*When Life and Beliefs Collide*, 146)

7. When the storms of life thrash us, what can we know from Proverbs 10:25, 30? Are you enduring a storm right now? How do you feel as you read these words?

Table Talk

for small group discussion use

Directions for use: During discussion time, the leader will use this guide to lead her group through an analysis of Psalm 91.

The book of Psalms: The book of Psalms is a compilation of prayers put to song. Some of the one hundred fifty psalms date from a thousand years before Christ. Many ancient cultures had psalms, but those are now found in museums as relics of the past, whereas the Israelites' hymns are still used today all over the world as a living language of prayer. Psalm 91 is similar to Psalm 90. Therefore, some attribute Moses, the author of Psalm 90, to also be the author of Psalm 91. Others believe the author may be

King David. Regardless, it is a poetic song about trust and protection in the Lord Most High.

To hear what the Holy Spirit is saying to you through this passage, you must ask some questions to help you observe the facts: Who? What? Where? Why? and How? No detail is too small. God loves for us to dig for treasures in his Word. This process of observing is very important and shouldn't be rushed. It is through this process that you see and discover what the author is saying. Many questions may come to mind as you read and reread. Ask them, write them down, and look up other Scripture passages to see what you can find. You may also want to read the passage in another version of the Bible.

—————— What Does the Passage Say? ——————

- *Who* is speaking in this passage? (Hint: There are two different speakers.)

- *What* four names of God did the psalmist choose to use (91:1–2)?

- *Where* is the psalmist? (Describe his position/location.)

- *What* does the psalmist's location afford him? (Describe all the ways in which he is protected.)

- *How* does the psalmist feel?

- *What* action did he take?

- *What* key words are in verse 1? (Hint: Try to find them elsewhere in the psalm.)

- *What* are the proclamations of each speaker (91:2, 14)?

- *How* many times does the word *I* appear in verses 14–16?

- *What* other details do you observe?

Now that you have read and thought and questioned and gathered all sorts of facts and clues like an investigative reporter, it's time to move to the next step: interpretation.

─────────────── **What Does It Mean?** ───────────────

- *Why* do you think the psalmist felt protected?

- *What* role, if any, did he play in being protected?

- *Why* do you think the Lord spoke in verse 14?

- *What* do you think is the main idea of the passage?

- *What* do you think the psalmist meant by "no harm will overtake you" (91:10)?

- *What* did you learn from this passage?

These kinds of questions will help you better understand what the author intended. Interpretation is key in moving to the next question, "What is the Holy Spirit saying to *me* through this passage?" Now move from seeing and understanding to applying God's Word to your life.

- *What* is the Holy Spirit saying to me in this psalm?

- *What* is one way to apply what he is saying to my life (i.e., family, friendships, marriage, work, ministry, social life)?

A Ring in a Pig's Nose

A Study on Discernment and Discretion

Remember when you watched a woman respond to a situation with keen insight? She was able to read the character and attitudes of people involved. She quickly distinguished shades of meaning and saw beyond the obvious and superficial. She detected what was really going on, and understood what was true from what was false and what was right from what was wrong. Then she responded with wise choices and sound judgment.

Would you like to be a woman like that—a woman who knows how to negotiate and navigate her way in the world? We call her mature. The Bible calls her wise, discerning, and discreet. Discretion is discernment in action—the behavior, speech, and conduct of a discerning woman. We all admire women like this. Some of us think this is a special gift, inaccessible to ordinary people. We are wrong. It is God's desire and design that we all be discerning women who live discreet lives. Let's find out how!

AN OPEN INVITATION

1. Where does discernment come from (Proverbs 2:6)?

OPTIONAL

Memorize Proverbs 11:22
Like a gold ring in a pig's snout is a beautiful woman who shows no discretion.

The capacity to recognize the voice of God through the ministry of the Holy Spirit arises out of friendship with God that is sustained through prayer, silent listening and attentiveness to all that is going on outside us, inside us, and between us and God. Through practice and experience we become familiar with the tone of God's voice, the content of his communications with us and his unique way of addressing us. We learn to recognize God's voice just as we recognize the voice of a loved one on the other end of the phone. There is a place deep inside each of us where God's Spirit witnesses with our spirit about things that are true (Rom. 8:16). It takes experience and practice to learn to recognize the communication that goes on in that place.
—Ruth Haley Barton
(*Invitation*, 119)

DIGGING DEEPER

Observe, interpret, and apply 1 Corinthians 2. What more do you discover about the source of wisdom and discernment?

DIGGING DEEPER

Women in Corinth were instructed to wear head coverings in church (1 Corinthians 11:3–16). Why? How did head coverings illustrate a woman's discretion in that culture? How does a woman exhibit discretion in our culture today? Although discernment is a gift of God, it is not free. There are several requirements. As you study, ask yourself, "Am I willing to pay the price in order to become discerning?"

2. Wisdom has prepared a banquet. Who is invited? Are you? What will you gain if you partake (9:1–6)?

3. What will you be called if you pursue wisdom (16:21)?

4. Are you discerning? Are you able to perceive what is going on around you with keen insight, distinguishing right from wrong and truth from error? If so, how do you think you learned discernment? If not, what hinders you?

5. Solomon became king over Israel as a youth. How was he feeling? What was the first thing he did (1 Kings 3:7–9)? How did God answer him (3:12)?

6. What is the request in Psalm 119:125? Is this the desire of your heart? If so, pray right now that God would give you a discerning heart. Use this space to record your prayer.

7. What else do you need to do to gain discernment (Proverbs 5:1–2; 8:34)?

Wisdom is divinely wrought in those, and only those, who apply themselves to God's revelation. . . . It is to be feared that many today who profess to be Christ's never learn wisdom, through failure to attend sufficiently to God's written word. . . . Do you spend as much time with the Bible each day as you do even with the newspaper? What fools some of us are!—and we remain fools all our lives, simply because we will not take the trouble to do what has to be done to receive the wisdom which is God's free gift. —J. I. Packer (*Knowing God*, 91)

8. Describe the heart attitude required (2:1–5; 23:23).

9. What other prerequisite to acquire wisdom do you find in 13:10 and 17:10? What is your attitude when this happens to you? Why is this necessary for the discerning?

10. Do you know anyone who refuses to learn from her mistakes? Is this true of you? What is your attitude when you fail? What can you learn from Proverbs 19:25?

11. How does a discerning woman add to her abilities (9:9)? Are you willing to be a lifelong learner?

12. What else is required to attain discernment (3:7; 8:13; 14:12; 19:16)?

13. Look back over the prerequisites for gaining wisdom. What is the most difficult for you? Are you willing to pay the price? How might you gain victory in this area of your life? Don't be afraid to ask the group for help.

DIGGING DEEPER

Read Philippians 1:9–11. What did the apostle Paul pray for believers? How do you feel knowing that this great man of faith sought wisdom on your behalf?

Choices. Life is full of them. We have to make them, but every choice we make brings risks. The Greek word we translate as *choice* is *hairesis*. It is also the word we translate as a *tenet* or a *heresy*. We cannot make our choices lightly because a choice can lead us into heresy. . . . We turn to the Word of God, the Bible, for help in making wise decisions. Our only sure anchor is the Scriptures, God's infallible Word. There we can learn by precept and by example.
—Alice Mathews
(*A Woman*, 11)

14. Describe the life of the discerning woman (Proverbs 2:7–12). Is this your life?

Not to decide is to decide.
—Harvey Cox
(Cory, *Quotable*, 96)

15. What's another benefit of a discerning life (3:21–23)?

It is interesting that Elijah never asked for guidance; guidance simply came in the context of his willingness to be with God in utter openness and vulnerability. Something in the willingness to stop the flow of his own words and listen in silence opened up space for the One who longs to speak and offer guidance for our next steps and knottiest questions. Like a wise and loving parent who waits for a self-sufficient or willful teenager to come to the end of her own wisdom and express openness to be guided, God loves us enough to wait for the teachable moments.
—Ruth Haley Barton
(*Invitation*, 117)

16. How will your words be affected (10:13)?

17. What else can you expect (12:2)? What do you think this means?

The Scriptures are full of examples of discerning women. If you want to learn more about them, read Alice Mathew's book *A Woman God Can Lead: Lessons from Women of the Bible Help You Make Today's Choices*.

18. What kind of student of the Word will you become (14:6; 17:24)?

19. What skill will you develop in your personal relationships (28:11)?

Sara colored my hair super-bright platinum and chocolate brown and almost every color in between. She gave me her lasagna recipe and also one of the best pieces of advice I've ever received. I was trying to figure out what to do next, worried about what people would think if I did this or that. And she said, "You know, Shauna, people really aren't thinking about you as often as you think they are." Huh. I can't tell you how many times I've repeated that to myself since she said it.

—Shauna Niequist
(*Bittersweet*, 195)

20. How will wise husbands perceive discerning wives (12:4)?

DISCRETION IS DISCERNMENT IN ACTION

To walk in the truth is more than to give assent to it. It means to apply it to one's behavior. He who "walks in the truth" is an integrated Christian in whom there is no dichotomy between profession and practice. On the contrary, there is in him an exact correspondence between his creed and his conduct.
—John Stott
(Swindoll, *Tale*, 589)

21. *Read Proverbs 11:22.* This is a wonderful little proverb that helps us understand truth. Can you figure out the analogy?

 Discerning Women (*2:52 minutes*). You are God's beautiful, precious creature. Believe it! Live it! And share that truth with other women in your life.

22. A discerning woman is discreet. Proverbs 7:11 gives us a bad example, showing us what a discreet woman is not! What do you learn? Does this mean a discreet woman says nothing and always stays home? What is the point of the verse?

God forbid that we should traffic in unlived truth.
—H. A. Ironside
(Swindoll, *Tale*, 589)

DIGGING DEEPER

First Timothy 2:9–10 describes a discreet woman in the first century church in Ephesus. How would the meaning of these verses translate to today? Describe a discreet woman in *our* culture.

DIGGING DEEPER

Abigail is a portrait of a discerning woman who exhibited discreet behavior that saved lives. Study 1 Samuel 25 and analyze the character of this outstanding woman.

When Aleksandr Solzhenitsyn was awarded the Nobel Prize in literature, he concluded his speech by quoting a Russian proverb: "One word of truth outweighs the whole world." If I could change a couple of words in that proverb, I would say, "One person of truth impacts the whole world."
—Charles Swindoll (*Tale*, 589)

WHAT HAVE YOU LEARNED?

23. Summarize what you have learned about discernment and discretion. Are you serious about making the changes needed for you to become a woman of wisdom and discernment—that is, a woman who understands how the world works and can influence it for good? How could your life be different as you passionately pursue these goals?

The Subtle Sin of Pride   LESSON 6

How would you identify someone who is proud? How do proud people act? Proud people boast and name drop. They feel superior because of what they drive, where they live, and what they wear. Proud people are narcissistic and selfish. They think the whole world revolves around them. It is easy to recognize these people as proud.

But pride is also a subtle heart attitude that sneaks up and grabs us before we know it. Pride can take a variety of forms: insisting on our own way, believing we are indispensable to God's work, and thinking that different is wrong. Pride is bashing someone's reputation, even subtly, and enjoying it. Pride is thinking we alone know how to fix everyone else. Proud people see others' faults clearly but expect others to understand that they "just had a bad day." Proud people expect grace but seldom extend it.

Pride is who we are without complete dependence on God. It is the mature Christian's Achilles' heel. It is the natural state of our flesh and most of us disguise it effectively. Often it is only those who live with us that know we have a pride problem. And we *all* do if we are not intentional about combating our natural tendency toward pride. That is why the Bible, and specifically Proverbs, warn us over and over to identify and eradicate the subtle sin of pride.

Sneaky, sneaky pride. When God blesses you or opens a door and you think you did it yourself, you are proud. If you are judgmental, you are proud. If it's your way or the highway, you are proud. If you think you are humble, you are proud. Let's get real and deal with our pride. When we do, our attitudes will change and that will change everything.

 Make a Name for Jesus (*3:19 minutes*). How do we enjoy our accomplishments without giving in to that awful Achilles' heel of the human existence—pride? Consider who you're making a name for.

OPTIONAL
_____

Memorize Proverbs 16:18
Pride goes before destruction, a haughty spirit before a fall.

Humility is not about putting yourself down. It's about a proper relationship with God. Look up to God. When we say "I can do this," we take God out of it and fail to acknowledge his existence. We become the focus. When we say "I can't," we take God out of it and fail to acknowledge his strength. We deflate ourselves or inflate ourselves, and both are wrong. We are not the source of air. God is. When we allow him to inflate us through his encouragement and deflate us through his discipline, we start all our sentences with God. We must acknowledge God.
—Susan Lawrence
(*Pure Emotion*, 180)

For the truth is that God in His wisdom, to make and keep us humble and to teach us to walk by faith, has hidden from us almost everything that we should like to know about the providential purposes which He is working out in the churches and in our own lives. "As thou knowest not what is the way of the wind, nor how the bones do grow in the womb of her that is with child; even so thou knowest not the work of God who doeth all" Ecclesiastes 11:5.
—J. I. Packer (*Knowing God*, 96)

One the repulsive manifestations of pride, *egotism* is the practice of thinking and speaking of oneself, of magnifying one's attainments and relating everything to self rather than to God and God's people.
—J. Oswald Sanders (*Spiritual Leadership*, 154)

1. How does God feel about our pride (Proverbs 8:13; 21:4)?

2. In 6:16–19, Solomon lists seven things the Lord hates. What tops the list? Try to imagine this picture and explain why you think this is so serious to God.

3. How do proud people view themselves (26:12)? When are you tempted to see yourself this way?

4. How does pride affect relationships (13:10; 17:19)? Can you recall a time when pride led to conflict in a relationship? How can we be peacemakers and enjoy harmony with others?

Whenever I'm tempted to become self-important and authoritative, I'm reminded of what the mother whale said to her baby: *"When you get to the top and start to 'blow,' that's when you get harpooned!"*
—James Dobson
(Swindoll, *Tale*, 174)

5. How does God deal with proud people (3:34; 16:5)?

6. What other consequences can we expect (11:2; 15:25; 16:18)?

7. What will happen in time if we vanquish our pride (29:23)? If you have observed this, share the incident with the group. (No names, please!)

PROBE THE PASSAGE

Throughout Jesus' years on earth, he honored humble people and humbled the proud. This week, let's "wring out" a New Testament passage that contains wonderful lessons on pride and humility. Trust the Holy Spirit to translate and explain this passage to you as you study throughout the week.

Commit to reading Luke 18:9–14 at least five days this week. Before you read each day, ask the Holy Spirit to illuminate the passage for you. During the week, as you meditate on the passage, ask yourself questions:

- What is going on in the parable?
- How do the two characters in the parable contrast?
- Why did Jesus tell this parable?
- What is the main point of the parable?
- Was there an idea that was particularly striking, causing me to stop and think?
- Why did God record this in the Bible for me?
- How does this impact my life right now and in the future?
- What questions do I have about this parable?

Don't be discouraged if nothing jumps out at you immediately. Be patient and keep probing the passage with questions. Record your thoughts each day.

Day 1

Day 2

Most often, pride grows out of an incomplete focus on the wonder and majesty of God, and from taking for granted his grace and blessings. Rooting myself in the truth of who God is—and who I am as his child— brings me to a grounded place of genuine humility.
—Nancy Beach (*Gifted*, 36)

Humility establishes our position in relation to God. God doesn't want you to put yourself down . . . just as he doesn't want you to build yourself up. He wants you to see yourself the way he sees you.

So God created human beings in his image. In the image of God he created them. He created them male and female. Genesis 1:27

As God's creation, you reflect him. You will never be as great as God, and yet he desires to draw you closer and closer to him despite your imperfections.
—Susan Lawrence (*Pure Emotion*, 180)

Day 3

Day 4

DIGGING DEEPER

Jesus is our prime example of humility. Study Philippians 2:5–11 and explain why.

DIGGING DEEPER

James also writes with conviction on the subject of humility. What principles do you discover in James 2:1–13?

Day 5

DIGGING DEEPER

Matthew reveals three ways we often exhibit spiritual pride in 6:1–16. What are they and how can we avoid these pitfalls?

DIGGING DEEPER

John 15 paints a picture of the spiritual life that will protect us from pride. What is the picture and what can you learn that will keep you humble?

8. What are specific ways to counteract pride (Proverbs 27:1–2; Philippians 2:3–5)? Share with the group your successes or defeats as you wrestle with pride. What have you learned?

Nothing is more distasteful to God than self-conceit. This first and fundamental sin in essence aims at enthroning self at the expense of God. . . . Pride is a sin of whose presence its victim is least conscious. . . . If we are honest, when we measure ourselves by the life of our Lord who humbled Himself even to death on a cross, we cannot but be overwhelmed with the tawdriness and shabbiness, and even the vileness, of our hearts.

—J. Oswald Sanders
(Swindoll, *Tale*, 468)

for small group discussion use

Directions for use: During discussion time, the leader will use this guide to lead her group through an analysis of Luke 18:9–14.

The Gospel of Luke: Early Christian writings identify the physician Luke as the author of this book and the book of Acts. Luke was a Gentile who never met Jesus but heard about him through the apostle Paul. Luke wrote this book around A.D. 60–62. It was written to a Gentile named Theophilus to reassure him that God was still at work in the Christian community after Christ's ascension.

To hear what the Holy Spirit is saying to you through this passage, you must ask questions to help you observe the facts: Who? What? Where? Why? and How? No detail is too small. God loves for us to dig for treasures in his Word. This process of observing is very important and shouldn't be rushed. It is through this process that you see and discover what the author is saying. Many questions may come to mind as you read and reread. Ask them, write them down, and look up other Scripture references to see what you can find. You may also want to read the passage in another version of the Bible.

——— What Does the Passage Say? ———

- *Who* is speaking in this passage?

- *Who* is being spoken to?

- *Who* are the people mentioned in this passage?

- *What* details can you observe about each of their lives? (Be sure to observe 18:11.)

- *Where* does the action take place?

- *Why* are the men there?

- *What* is happening in the passage? (Look for action words.)

- *How* would you describe the scene?

- *What* statements are made by the men? (List them in order.)

- *What* contrast do you observe in the statements?

- *How* many times is the pronoun "I" used in verses 11–12?

- *What* statement did Jesus make?

- *How* would you describe the reaction of each man upon hearing Jesus' statement?

- *What* does the word *justified* mean?

Now that you have read and thought and questioned and gathered all sorts of facts and clues like an investigative reporter, it's time to move to the next step: interpretation.

―――――――――――――― **What Does It Mean?** ――――――――――――――

- *Why* do you think the Pharisee listed his "dos and don'ts"?

- *Why* do you think the tax collector approached God as he did?

- *Why* do you think Jesus contrasted these two men?

- *What* could be a modern-day equivalent?

- *Why* do you think Jesus made the statement in verse 14?

- *What* do you think is the main idea of the passage?

- *What* did you learn from this passage?

These kinds of questions will help you better understand what the author meant in the passage. Interpretation is key in moving to the next question, "What is the Holy Spirit saying to me through this passage?" Now move from seeing and understanding to applying God's Word to your life.

- *What* is the Holy Spirit saying to me in this passage?

- *What* is one way to apply what he's saying to my life (perhaps to my family relationships, friendships, marriage, work, ministry, or social life)?

Money Talk | LESSON 7

OPTIONAL
_____

Memorize 1 Timothy
6:10–11

For the love of money is a
root of all kinds of evil. Some
people, eager for money,
have wandered from the faith
and pierced themselves with
many griefs. But you, . . .
flee from all this, and pursue
righteousness, godliness,
faith, love, endurance and
gentleness.

Are you rich or poor? How do you measure wealth and poverty? Is it the size of your bank account or the depth of your relationships? Is it a joyride in your car or that joyful feeling of giving the Lord your best? Most Christians would describe the latter as a true picture of wealth. Nevertheless, we all need money to live. That's the way the world works.

Our attitude toward money matters. Some women among us never worry about money; others worry about money every day. Why? God has blessed some with material resources and has withheld it from others, possibly for a particular purpose—a lesson we need to learn or as a means to glorify himself. Some are poor because they have been irresponsible stewards. Yet, as we look around the world, we cannot find a reason why Americans own so much of the material wealth of the world and those in third-world countries barely survive. We probably will never find the answer to the question, "Why do some have so much and others so little?"

But whatever our individual situation today, the Bible reveals principles about money to help us all. Proverbs is packed full of insight into the world of money—those greenbacks in our wallet that determine where we live, what we wear, and many of our opportunities to enjoy life. What heart attitude about money pleases God? How can we enjoy wealth regardless of our bank account? And what are the advantages and challenges of having money? Let's dig into a common subject that can be a tool for blessings or destruction!

The secret is keeping our worldly goods in spiritual perspective and maintaining a healthy balance.
—Jill Briscoe (*8 Choices*, 41)

1. Agur prayed that God would bless him materially. What is the state of true material blessing? What is the danger of riches? What is the danger of poverty (Proverbs 30:7–9)?

Materialism is one of the most powerful pseudo gods in our culture. When we think of the word materialism in everyday conversation, we think of going shopping, collecting possessions, owning status symbols, dressing for success, and owning all the right toys. . . . But if we look deeper into our souls, we find that materialism is the tangible evidence that we use, at times, to replace the Unseen, the Intangible, the Holy Other.
—David Allen (*Shattering*, 69)

Where is the life we have lost in living, where is the wisdom we have lost in knowledge?
—T. S. Eliot (*Chorus from the Rock*, 121)

2. Have you experienced either extreme? Do you agree with Agur? Share your story if you want to.

3. Does God value the rich more than the poor, or vice versa? Explain your answer (22:2; John 3:16).

DIGGING DEEPER

What are the timeless truths about money in Matthew 6:19–21, 24, 31–34?

4. Money itself is not evil. We need money to live, and we are admonished to work hard to provide for ourselves and our loved ones. Nevertheless, when is money dangerous and what can happen (1 Timothy 6:10)?

"Success" and social standing and . . . economic power . . . is the god of many people in the highly competitive Western culture, and it does what every ultimate concern must do: it demands unconditional surrender to its laws even if the price is the sacrifice of genuine human relations, personal conviction and [creativity]. Its threat is social and economic defeat and its promise—indefinite as all such promises—the fulfillment of one's being.
—Paul Tillich
(*Dynamics of Faith*, 4)

 The Trap (*3:57 minutes*). Stuff is a trap that sidetracks us from what God wants to do in our lives. Hear Sue's true confessions.

5. Proverbs reveals some advantages to having money. What are they?

Proverbs 14:20

Proverbs 18:23

Proverbs 22:7

6. There are also disadvantages to having money. What are they?

Proverbs 11:28

Proverbs 13:8

Proverbs 18:11

In Proverbs, Solomon groups people into categories—the "righteous" rich, the "righteous" poor, and the wicked. He comments on their circumstances and teaches lessons for each group. Let's see what we can learn about each group.

7. What does Solomon instruct us to do in Proverbs 3:9? What do you think this means? What are some ways to do this?

Is it possible that our technological developments have moved so fast that they have outdistanced our ethical decision making? Now we are faced with the possibility of cloning the human embryo. . . . Technology can serve humankind as a means of enhancing personal dignity. We cannot, however, allow it to become a pseudo god where it becomes an end in itself, and thus destroys human beings.
—David Allen (*Shattering*, 69)

8. Our natural tendency is to hold on to what we have. But Solomon reveals a principle showing us how the world works in 3:10 and 11:24. (See also Ecclesiastes 11:1.) What is the principle?

If we suspect we are addicted to money or to the possession of what we can buy, we need to develop the habit of regularly giving some of those riches away. Ask yourself if you have developed a real attachment to some possessions or other. Look around to see if someone needs that particular thing more than you do. Pray about it. If you are honest, you may realize that the thing has you in its power. Give it away speedily!
—Jill Briscoe (*8 Choices*, 39)

9. Is this a promise that God will bless us if we use our money for God's work? Is God obliged to pay us back? Discuss.

10. Wisdom speaks in Proverbs 8:17–21. What are some of the benefits of loving God and pursuing wisdom? Does this mean that God sometimes blesses his beloved with money? Does he always? What other kinds of blessings does he bestow that are "better than fine gold"?

11. Describe the picture of the "righteous" rich in 14:24.

12. When God blesses his beloved with money, what else does he do (10:22)?

13. With money comes great responsibility. Why has God given his beloved money? What are the "righteous" rich to do with their money?

Proverbs 11:25

Proverbs 11:26

Proverbs 14:31

Proverbs 19:17

DIGGING DEEPER

Who are the New Testament men and women who changed their focus in life from making money to following Jesus? List them. What did they give up? What did they gain? What can you learn from them?

When you fix your eyes on things invariably it leads to materialism. You fix your eyes on things and you will continually be attracted to gadgets, money, an abundance of the plastic, chrome, metal, wood, all the elements about us. You will continually be dissatisfied. The millionaire, John D. Rockefeller, was asked one time, "How much does it take to satisfy a man completely?" He said," It take a little bit more than he has."
—Spiros Zodhiates
(Swindoll, *Tale*, 392)

The terms "rich" and "poor" are relative. Let's use the term "poor" to refer to those who are uncertain about having the resources to meet their future needs. Often God withholds money from his beloved. Jesus, Paul, and others owned almost nothing and depended on charity for daily necessities. Third-world Christians live in modest conditions, some even in squalor. There is little equity in the world today. Does this mean that God does not love the "righteous" poor?

14. According to Solomon, what is better than an abundance of money?

Proverbs 15:16

Proverbs 15:17

Jesus talked about money. One-sixth of the Gospels, and one-third of the parables address the subject of stewardship. Jesus was no fund-raiser. He dealt with money matters, however, because money matters. It's a surprise to many people, Christians included, that the Bible has so much to say about this subject.
—Charles Swindoll (*Tale*, 231)

Proverbs 22:1

Proverbs 28:6

Summarize the main idea of these four proverbs.

15. What quality do the "righteous" poor often develop (28:11)? Why?

16. The "righteous" poor must work hard every day for the basic necessities. What is the result according to 10:16? What are the benefits of working hard for what you enjoy?

> If a person gets his attitude toward money straight, it will help straighten out almost every other area of his life.
> —Billy Graham
> (Cory, *Quotable*, 250)

17. *Read Proverbs 15:6.* What treasures do you think can be found in the home of the "righteous" poor?

> Money has never yet made anyone rich.
> —Seneca (Cory, *Quotable*, 254)

18. Solomon talks about two kinds of people in 13:7. Who are they and what can be true about each?

THE WICKED

19. What is the wicked person's attitude toward money (28:20)? Where is her focus? Contrast this attitude with the heart of the righteous.

20. Why is the covetous woman a fool (23:4–5)?

21. What is she forgetting (11:4; 13:21)?

22. How do the wicked rich use their money? What results (22:16; 28:22)?

23. What happens to dishonest gain? In contrast, how can the righteous be good stewards (13:11)?

24. What ultimately happens to the wicked person's wealth?

Proverbs 13:22

Proverbs 28:8

25. Which group are you—the righteous rich, the righteous poor, or the wicked? Compare your situation to others in America, then others worldwide.

26. Analyze the way you use money. Do you think God is pleased?

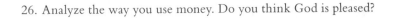

Beyond giving our material possessions, God calls upon us to give ourselves away—our time, energy, and passion. One way to develop a generosity of spirit is to get involved with missions.
—Jill Briscoe (*8 Choices*, 41)

27. What is your attitude toward money? How has this affected your walk with the Lord? If you love money, confess this attitude and ask God to change your heart. Devise a plan that reflects a new heart.

When we come into the Church, we take upon ourselves the vows of our holy Christianity, vows more solemn than any oath in any earthly court. Before the Lord, and the great congregation, we renounce the devil and all his works—the vain pomp and glory of the world—and consecrate our souls and bodies as a living sacrifice to God and accept publicly the Scriptures as the rule of our life and practice.
—Annie Wittenmyer, *Woman's Work for Jesus* (1871)

28. What do you think God wants you to learn from your current circumstance?

29. What have you learned from this lesson that might change the way you view or use the resources God has given you?

Life, Death, and Aging

Our media is obsessed with death. Given to extremes, the television, film, and video game industries blow up a million people without hesitation. Americans, as an audience, have become numb. Death on the screen is so common we hardly pay attention. In contrast, discussing the reality of our own death or of those we love is taboo. Americans talk about sex much more often than they talk about death.

The Bible addresses the subject of life and death. The Old Testament saints did not have the full understanding of eternal life that the New Testament has provided us. They did not know that God would send his Son, Jesus, to die for our sins, and change the way we view death. Even so, death is still our enemy—ugly, satanic, destroying our bodies and desecrating our loved ones.

In this lesson, we will first learn about life and death from an Old Testament perspective as we study Proverbs and other Old Testament books. Then we'll expand our study to New Testament teachings on life and death. Through the study of both views, we can learn to love life, live well today, and not fear the future!

OPTIONAL

Memorize John 10:10

The thief comes only to steal and kill and destroy; I have come that they may have life, and have it to the full.

My dear friend's mother-in-law moved into their home because of health concerns. The elderly woman was discouraged and kept saying, "I don't know why Jesus keeps me here. I'd rather go to heaven to be with Him." But my friend shared her answer with me: "God keeps her here to teach me patience and unconditional love—the kind of love Jesus has for us all." Yes, I thought. God has His purposes, often beyond our understanding. How marvelous are His ways! And how grateful I am for wise friends. —Sue

Solomon celebrates life in the book of Proverbs. To him, life is more than mere existence. It is flourishing while enjoying rich relationships with God and others. Let's examine some word pictures that speak of the wonder of life.

Abundant Life

1. What kind of life does God want for you? Why is it so important that you seek wisdom (Proverbs 3:13–18)?

2. How does David describe the abundant life (Psalm 36:7–9)?

> Life with God is a daring dream, full of flashes and last-minute exits and generally all the things we've said we'll never do. And with the surprises comes great hope.
> —Shauna Niequist (*Cold Tangerines*, 207)

> Man alone . . . has foreknowledge of his coming death . . . and, possessing this foreknowledge, has a chance, if he chooses to take it, of pondering over the strangeness of his destiny. . . . [He] has at least a possibility of coping with it, since he is endowed with the capacity to think about it in advance and . . . to face it and deal with it in some way that is worthy of human dignity.
> —Arnold Toynbee ("Traditional Attitudes Towards Death," 63)

3. What is the source of abundant life (Proverbs 8:35; 14:30)?

4. What is necessary to obtain abundant life (13:14)? Picture the analogy. What is Solomon revealing?

5. What else is described as a "tree of life" (13:12; 15:4)? Recall a time when you experienced these "trees of life."

6. Are you enjoying an abundant life? If so, thank God. If not, what is missing? Look back at the previous verses. Are you looking somewhere else for life? Discuss.

Extending Life

God is sovereign and knows the choices we will make and how long we will live. However, it is also true that our choices matter and affect our lives in many ways.

7. What do Proverbs 3:1–2, 4:10, 9:11, and 10:27 reveal about our conduct and the length of our lives?

8. Have you ever observed someone making destructive choices that brought disaster? If so, please share the story with the group. (No names, please.)

DIGGING DEEPER

Do a character study on the first king of Israel, Saul. His life is recorded in 1 Samuel, beginning in chapter 8. Make a chart of his choices and the consequences. How did he bring death upon himself?

9. What is Solomon's command in Proverbs 9:6?

It's rebellious, in a way, to choose joy, to choose to dance, to choose to love your life. It's much easier and much more common to be miserable.
—Shauna Niequist (*Cold Tangerines*, 234)

Preparation for old age should begin not later than one's teens. A life which is empty of purpose until 65 will not suddenly become filled on retirement.
—Arthur Morgan (Cory, *Quotable*, 17)

10. Are you behaving in a manner that might shorten your life? What do you need to do to stop? Are you failing to behave in a manner that might lengthen your life? What do you need to do to start?

Facing Death

Only those who have faced death can live well.

11. What does Solomon say about the day of death in Ecclesiastes 7:1–4? Why do you think he insists that it is wise to face death?

12. Solomon warns us to follow wisdom's ways so that we avoid premature and unnecessary physical death, which can be the consequence of foolish behavior. What does he warn us against in Proverbs 9:13–18? (See also 2:16–19 and 5:3–6.)

> We may be frankly bewildered at things that happen to us, but God knows exactly what He is doing, and what He is after, in His handling of our affairs. Always, and in everything, He is wise: we shall see that hereafter, even where we never saw it here. . . . Meanwhile, we ought not to hesitate to trust His wisdom, even when He leaves us in the dark.
> —J. I. Packer
> (*Knowing God*, 87)

13. What happens when we refuse to discipline those under our guidance (19:18; 23:14)?

14. What happens when we refuse to follow God's direction and instead insist on our own way (14:12; 21:16)?

> Man is born with his hands clenched; he dies with his hands wide open. Entering life he desires to grasp everything; leaving the world, all he possessed has slipped away.
> —*The Talmud*

Facing Old Age

The process of aging makes death a reality.

For the ignorant, old age is as winter; for the learned, it is a harvest.
—Jewish Proverb
(Cory, *Quotable*, 19)

15. How do Proverbs 16:31 and 20:29 portray getting older?

The seven ages of man: spills, drills, thrills, bills, ills, pills, wills.
—Richard J. Needham
(Cory, *Quotable*, 19)

16. Are you feeling the aging process yet? If so, how do you feel about getting older?

17. How do you treat older people? Do you think God agrees with our culture's devaluation of the elderly?

DIGGING DEEPER

There are parts of aging that are painful and hard to bear. Study Solomon's portrait of aging in Ecclesiastes 12:1–7. What analogies does he use to describe what happens when we get older? What is his advice to the aging?

Hope in the Old Testament

18. What did Solomon know about death (Proverbs 12:28; 14:32)?

In the central places of every heart there is a recording chamber; so long as it receives messages of beauty, hope, cheer, and courage, so long are you young. When the wires are all down and your heart is covered with the snows of pessimism and the ice of cynicism, then, and then only, are you grown old.
—General Douglas MacArthur, on his 75th birthday (Cory, *Quotable*, 19)

19. Old Testament authors taught lessons on life and death that are still valuable for us today. What is the lesson from Psalm 90:10, 12?

20. Have you learned to "number your days"? What does this mean for you this week? What do you need to do to pursue abundant living and avoid destructive consequences?

PART 2: LIFE AND DEATH IN THE NEW TESTAMENT

As New Testament believers we are privileged to know more about life and death than the Old Testament saints.

21. What truth do you discover from Hebrews 9:27? (The judgment there refers to the *bema*, the rewards ceremony for believers.)

22. What was Paul's attitude about life and death (Philippians 1:21)? Can you echo his sentiments? Why or why not?

23. What does Jesus reveal concerning eternal life after physical death (John 11:26)?

I'm sittin' on the edge of heaven, and His eye is still on me. I'm not afraid to die. I'm kinda looking forward to it. I know the Lord has His arms wrapped around this big fat sparrow.
—Ethel Waters (Knaack, *Ethel Waters*, 111)

Study the Gospels' accounts of the resurrection and crystallize the truths you learn in summary statements (Matthew 28; Mark 16; Luke 24; John 20:10–21:25). What do you learn about your new physical body from Jesus' resurrected body? To harmonize these accounts, read chapter 10, "The Resurrection of the King," in *The Words and Works of Jesus Christ* by J. Dwight Pentecost.

24. What will happen when Jesus returns to earth to claim you and give you a new physical body (1 Corinthians 15:51–57)? How do you feel as you read these verses?

25. How should we live while we wait (1 Corinthians 15:58)?

ARE YOU LIVING ABUNDANTLY?

 Preoccupied (*3:55 minutes*). Are you dissatisfied with your body? Or engaged in a constant pursuit to defy aging? Sue challenges us to keep a right balance between body care and soul care.

26. Are you free from the fear of death? Are you fully embracing the abundant life? What has Christ done for us to enable us to overcome our fear (Hebrews 2:14–15)? Express your praise to God for his wonderful gifts of abundant and eternal life.

A Portrait of Perfection

LESSON 9

Lessons from Superwoman

We all hate her—the woman who has it all and does it all perfectly. Fortunately, she isn't real! Nevertheless, it's good to look into the eyes of perfection and aim high.

Who is the Proverbs 31 woman? Every mother wants the perfect wife for her son, and King Lemuel's mother wrote about her dream daughter-in-law in the final chapter of Proverbs. She taught her son what to look for in a good woman. Her words were so wise that God made sure they were recorded for women (and suitors) of all eras.

She's our model. She's the superwoman of the tenth century B.C. Of course, we need to study her in light of her times, but we can still glean many truths about what it means to be a wise woman today. As we conclude our study of Proverbs, this section will help us evaluate our progress.

 Read Proverbs 31:10–31.

 Busy, Busy, Busy (*3:49 minutes*). What does *temperance* mean, and how can it help in a culture of extremes?

OPTIONAL
Memorize Proverbs 31:10

A wife of noble character who can find? She is worth far more than rubies.

The goal of Proverbs is to teach us to be wise. Throughout the book we hear that the fear of the Lord is the beginning of wisdom, that wisdom is a precious commodity, that wisdom is skill in living, and that we should seek it with all our hearts, minds, and strength. Solomon ends his book with a visual picture of wisdom and it's a woman! She is a beautiful example of all that we have been learning in our study. What a wonderful review and conclusion to our adventure in Proverbs.   —Sue

HER VALUE

1. What is the value of a wise and godly woman? How rare is she (31:10)?

2. As a Christian you are of tremendous value to God simply because you are his daughter. He loves you unconditionally. However, your attitude and actions determine your impact and influence for Christ. Over the past few weeks, we have been looking at various character qualities that make you wise. How would you assess your growth during this study? When it comes to influencing your world for Christ, what is your worth?

HER "SIGNIFICANT OTHER"

In Solomon's day almost everyone married. Women wed as young teens under the guidance of their family.

3. Describe her relationship with her husband (31:11–12). How do you think she treats him? What is her heart attitude?

4. What is her husband's status in the community (31:23)? How do you think she contributes? If you are married, what can you do (or not do) to honor your husband in public?

It's easy to read Proverbs 31 and conclude that our woman of worth never stopped working. But that isn't the case. Clearly she had a splendid relationship with her husband. . . . She also had a good relationship with her children. In verse 28 we learn that they rise up and call her blessed. She wasn't just a well-dressed dynamo in perpetual motion. She took time to build relationships and kindness was on her tongue.
—Alice Mathews
(*A Woman*, 168)

DIGGING DEEPER

Study Paul's mandate to families in Ephesians 5:21–6:4. Describe the heart attitude of husband and wife as they submit and sacrifice for each other. How is the relationship between husband and wife different from the relationship between children and parents? For more insight into the concept of headship, read *Men and Women in the Church* by Sarah Sumner.

Scholars have calculated that it took three to four hours every morning for women in Bible times to produce bread for the normal sized family.
—Miriam Feinberg Vamosh (*Women*, 14)

5. In her day, most everything was made from scratch. What is her attitude toward her work (31:13, 19)?

6. What kinds of meals do you think were on her table (31:14)?

7. What do you learn about her schedule from verse 15? Does this mean you must do this too? What do you think is the main point of the verse?

8. What do you learn about her household from the latter part of verse 15? How does this fact impact her everyday life? How do you feel about her now?

9. What is suggested in verses 16, 18, and 24? Does she work outside her home? If so, in what capacity?

We can gird ourselves with strength and dignity only when we have good handle on who we are and what we are about. We must concentrate our strength where it can make a difference for the important people in our lives. Clearly our Proverbs 31 woman of worth could best help her husband and provide for her family by buying fields, planting grapes, and making and selling sashes.
—Alice Mathews
(*A Woman*, 170)

10. What does verse 17 tell us about her physical fitness?

Weaving was only one part of the work that went into transforming sheep wool, goat hair, or plant fibers into cloth. For wool, the work began with the shearing of the animal. After the wool was cleaned and dyed, the threads would be spun on a spindle. The spindle was a short, narrow rod with a circular weight, known as the spindle whorl, attached to it. The whorl helped keep the rod in a vertical position and also was used to turn the rod on its axis. The spinner's deft and constant turning of the rod (harder than it looks!) transformed the raw fibers into thread of even thickness. Then came the weaving of the thread into cloth on an upright loom. Some of these looms have been found in archaeological excavations.
—Miriam Feinberg
Vamosh (*Women*, 17–18)

11. What was her particular ministry (31:20)? What is yours?

APPEARANCES

12. How is her family dressed (31:21)? How do you think they feel as a result?

13. How is she dressed (31:22)? How does a wise woman keep up appearances without focusing too much on externals? What is a good balance?

HER CHARACTER

14. According to the first part of verse 25, what is her finest outfit?

A perfectionist is one who takes great pains—and gives them to other people.
—*Education Digest*
(Cory, *Quotable*, 280)

15. Which is more important to you—an expensive wardrobe or wisdom? How do your calendar and checkbook reflect your priorities?

16. According to the second part of verse 25, what is the Proverbs 31 woman's attitude toward the future? What is yours? Why?

17. What characterizes her words (31:26)? Your words?

18. How would you rate her work ethic (31:27)?

HER REWARDS

19. What do her loved ones say about her (31:28–29)? What is the value of having loved ones speak this way about you? Do you think her children are grown? Why or why not?

20. What is the source of this woman's success? Why is this a fitting end to the book (31:30)?

21. Where else does she hear words of praise (31:31)? How does our work in our homes or jobs affect our influence for Christ in the community and world?

22. Do you think this woman made a significant difference in the world where she lived? What do you think they might have written on her tombstone?

No, I'm not the Proverbs 31 woman, but . . .

Remember, becoming a wise woman is a lifelong endeavor. God expects faithfulness but not perfection. Continue to seek him with all your heart and you will become a woman God can use to change the world.

23. Review the lessons in this guide. Evaluate your progress through this study. What has God been teaching you?

24. Where have you made significant progress? Where do you continue to struggle? (Ask God to reveal areas of growth and areas of weakness.)

25. Encourage the women in your group. Who has made you feel welcome? Who has ministered to you? Who have you appreciated and why? Who have you seen grow closer to the Lord? Who have you seen make progress? Be sure to tell these people.

Works Cited

Allen, David. *Shattering the Gods Within*. Chicago: Moody Press, 1994.

Barton, Ruth Haley. *Invitation to Solitude and Silence: Experiencing God's Transforming Presence*. Downers Grove, IL: InterVarsity Press, 2010.

Beach, Nancy. *Gifted to Lead: The Art of Leading as a Woman in the Church*. Grand Rapids: Zondervan, 2008.

Biehl, Bobb. *Mentoring*. Nashville: Broadman & Holman, 1996.

Brestin, Dee. *We Are Sisters*. Colorado Springs: Victor Books, 1994.

Briscoe, Jill. *8 Choices That Will Change a Woman's Life*. New York: Howard Books, 2004.

Carvalho, Corinne L. *Encountering Ancient Voices: A Guide to Reading the Old Testament*. Winona, MN: Saint Mary's Press, Christian Brothers Publications, 2006.

Cory, Lloyd. *Quotable Quotations*. Wheaton, IL: Victor Books, 1985.

DeMoss, Nancy Leigh. *A Place of Quiet Rest*. Chicago: Moody Press, 2000.

Eliot, T. S. *Chorus from the Rock in the Great Thoughts*. New York: Random House, 1985.

Evans, Rachel Held. "Women of Valor: It's About Character, Not Roles," blog post. June 11, 2012. http://rachelheldevans.com/mutuality -women-roles.

Gehring, Stephanie. "Wisdom," Relevant Magazine website. March 1, 2004. http://www.relevantmagazine.com/god/deeper-walk/features/ 584-wisdom.

Gorman, Julie. *Community That Is Christian*. Grand Rapids: Baker, 2002.

Hislop, Beverly. *Shepherding a Woman's Heart*. Chicago: Moody Publishers, 2003.

Hunt, Susan. *Spiritual Mothering*. Wheaton, IL: Crossway, 1992.

James, Carolyn Custis. *When Life and Beliefs Collide*. Grand Rapids: Zondervan, 2001.

Kenny, Sister Elizabeth. *And They Shall Walk*. London: Hale, 1951.

Knaack, Twila. *Ethel Waters: I Touched a Sparrow*. Dallas: Word, 1979.

Lamott, Anne. *Traveling Mercies*. New York: Pantheon Books, 1999.

Lawrence, Susan H. *Pure Emotion*. Bloomington, IN: WestBow Press, 2011.

Lucado, Max. *In the Grip of Grace*. Dallas: Word, 1996.

Mathews, Alice. *A Woman God Can Lead: Lessons from Women of the Bible Help You Make Today's Choices.* Grand Rapids: Discovery House, 1998.

Moore, Beth. *Get Out of That Pit: Straight Talk About God's Deliverance.* Nashville: Integrity, 2007.

Niequist, Shauna. *Bittersweet: Thoughts on Change, Grace, and Learning the Hard Way.* Grand Rapids: Zondervan, 2010.

Niequist, Shauna. *Cold Tangerines: Celebrating the Extraordinary Nature of Everyday Life.* Grand Rapids: Zondervan, 2007.

Packer, J. I. *Knowing God.* Downers Grove, IL: InterVarsity, 1973.

Paffenroth, Kim. *In Praise of Wisdom: Literary and Theological Reflections on Faith and Reason.* New York: Continuum, 2004.

Sanders, J. Oswald. *Spiritual Leadership: Principles of Excellence for Every Believer.* Text updated by Mark Fackler. Chicago: Moody Publishers, 1994.

Swindoll, Charles R. *Grace Awakening.* Dallas: Word, 1990.

Swindoll, Charles R. *Living on the Ragged Edge.* Waco, TX: Word, 1995.

Swindoll, Charles R. *Tale of the Tardy Oxcart.* Nashville: Word, 1998.

The Talmud. Translated by H. Polano (1876). San Diego: The Book Tree, 2003.

Taylor, Barbara Brown. *An Altar in the World: A Geography of Faith.* New York: HarperOne, 2009.

Tillich, Paul. *Dynamics of Faith.* New York: Perennial, 2001.

Toynbee, Arnold. "Traditional Attitudes Towards Death." *Man's Concern with Death*, ed. by Arnold Toynbee et al. New York: McGraw-Hill, 1968.

Vamosh, Miriam Feinberg. *Women at the Time of the Bible.* Israel: Herzlia, 2007.

Winner, Lauren. *Mudhouse Sabbath: An Invitation to a Life of Spiritual Discipline.* Brewster, MA: Paraclete Press, 2007.

Witt, Connie, and Cathi Workman. *That Makes Two of Us: Lifestyle Mentoring for Women.* Loveland, CO: Group, 2009.

About the Author

Sue Edwards is associate professor of Christian education (her specialization is women's studies) at Dallas Theological Seminary, where she has the opportunity to equip men and women for future ministry. She brings over thirty years of experience into the classroom as a Bible teacher, curriculum writer, and overseer of several megachurch women's ministries. As minister to women at Irving Bible Church and director of women's ministry at Prestonwood Baptist Church in Dallas, she has worked with women from all walks of life, ages, and stages. Her passion is to see modern and postmodern women connect, learn from one another, and bond around God's Word. Her Bible studies have ushered thousands of women all over the country and overseas into deeper Scripture study and community experiences.

With Kelley Mathews, Sue has coauthored *New Doors in Ministry to Women: A Fresh Model for Transforming Your Church, Campus, or Mission Field*; *Women's Retreats: A Creative Planning Guide*; and *Leading Women Who Wound: Strategies for an Effective Ministry*. Sue and Kelley joined with Henry Rogers to coauthor *Mixed Ministry: Working Together as Brothers and Sisters in an Oversexed Society*.

Sue has a doctor of ministry degree from Gordon-Conwell Theological Seminary in Boston and a master's in Bible from Dallas Theological Seminary. With Dr. Joye Baker, she oversees the Dallas Theological Seminary doctor of ministry degree in Christian education with a women-in-ministry emphasis.

Sue has been married to David for forty years. They have two married daughters, Heather and Rachel, and five grandchildren. David is a CAD applications engineer, a lay prison chaplain, and founder of their church's prison ministry.